insight text guide

Ross Walker

Generals Die in Bed

Charles Yale Harrison

First published in 2005, reprinted in 2008, 2016, 2020.

Insight Publications Pty Ltd
3/350 Charman Road
Cheltenham VIC 3192
Australia
Tel: +61 3 8571 4950
Fax: +61 3 8571 0257
Email: books@insightpublications.com.au

www.insightpublications.com.au

National Library of Australia Cataloguing-in-Publication data:
Walker, Ross.
Charles Yale Harrison's Generals Die in Bed : text guide.
For VCE English students.
9781921088001 (paperback)
1. Harrison, Charles Yale 1898 – 1954. Generals die in bed.
I. Title.
813.52

Other ISBNs:
9781922378897 (digital)
9781922378903 (bundle: print + digital)

Cover design: Gisela Beer, based on a concept by The Modern Art Production Group

Printed in Australia

contents

CHARACTER MAP

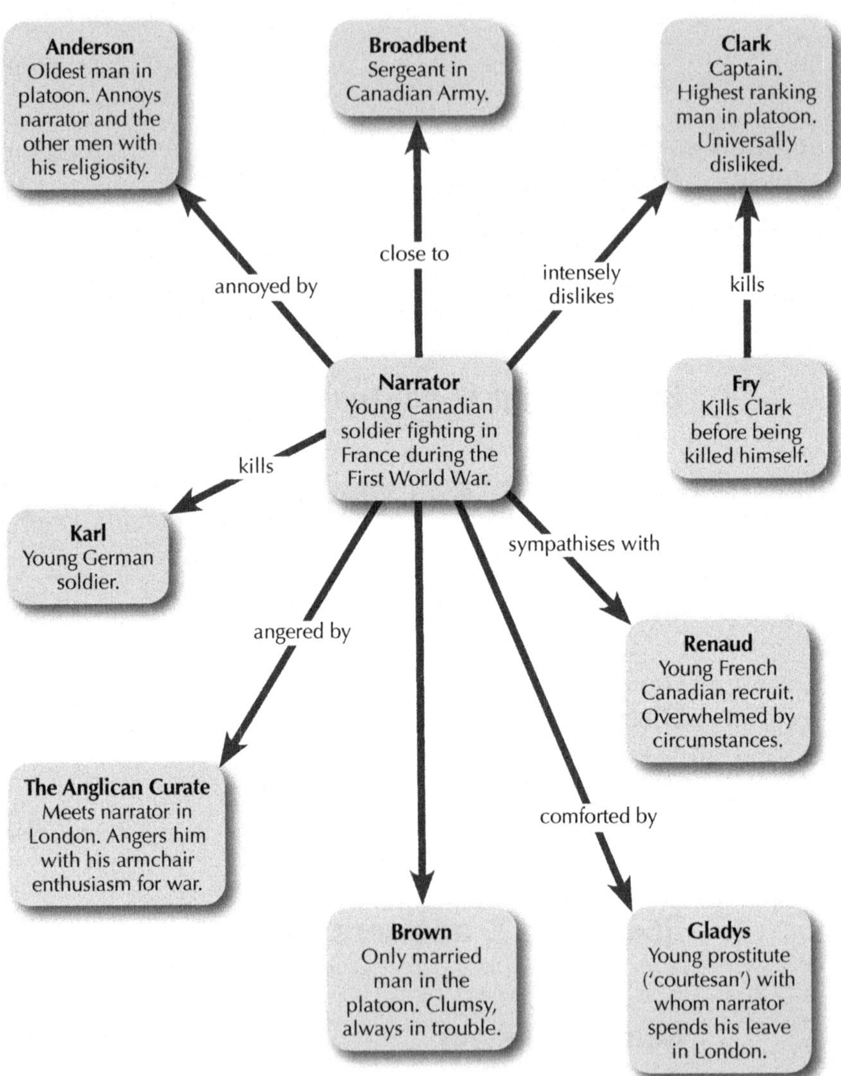

INTRODUCTION

First published in 1930, more than a decade after the conclusion of World War I, *Generals Die in Bed* draws its inspiration from the ordeal of the author, Charles Yale Harrison, as a young Canadian soldier serving in the trenches on the Western Front in France and Belgium. It describes his experiences from the time of his departure from Montreal, Quebec, to the time when he was wounded at the Battle of Amiens, on 8 August 1918, and released from the war. The main body of the narrative relates uncompromisingly the horrors of the war itself: the filth of the trenches, the misery of the men, the savagery of the fighting. It confirms the truth that this war was one of the most disastrous events of the twentieth century. And there is a special sadness in remembering that the lives of so many young men (many still teenage boys) came to an end in terrible circumstances, thousands of miles from their homes in countries such as Canada, Australia and New Zealand.

At about the same time as the publication of this novel, a spate of other works by writers who had served in World War I appeared. Among them were *All Quiet on the Western Front* by Erich Maria Remarque; *Goodbye to All That* by Robert Graves; *A Farewell to Arms* by Ernest Hemingway; *Memoirs of an Infantry Officer* by Siegfried Sassoon and *Her Privates We* by Frederic Manning. All these now classic novels and memoirs of the war appeared in the year 1929. We may surmise that the authors needed that decade-long distance from the events they had experienced before being able to bring themselves to put them down in writing. The same was true of veterans of the Vietnam War, much later, whose memoirs appeared at a similar distance from the end of that war. We can well imagine that the general public, too, at the time of each war, would have been thoroughly sick of the news and stories of war, and would have been unwilling to read further about the war until long after its end. Even now, nearly a century after its conclusion, the brutality and extraordinary waste of human life of World War I remain shocking, and *Generals Die in Bed* provides an unflinching testament both to its horrors and to its utter futility.

BACKGROUND & CONTEXT

The author

Charles Yale Harrison (1898–1954) was a Canadian author and World War I veteran. Though born in Philadelphia, he moved to Montreal as a child and grew up in Canada. At sixteen, he worked for the *Montreal Star* newspaper before joining the Royal Montreal Regiment to fight in Europe in World War I. He was repatriated after sustaining an injury to his foot in 1918, on the first day of the Battle of Amiens. Harrison took a variety of jobs after the war, working as a theatre manager in Montreal, and then as a journalist, author and public relations consultant in New York. He married three times and was survived by his third wife. *Generals Die in Bed* was his most successful novel.

Although *Generals Die in Bed* is not one of the best-known novels of World War I, it sparked considerable controversy in Canada when it first appeared. Many veterans were outraged at the allegations that members of the Royal Montreal Regiment had pillaged the town of Arras and killed prisoners. Some considered the allegations to be complete fabrications. One ex-soldier argued that 'though claimed by some advertisements as a genuine record of service, [the book] is obviously fiction of the blood-curdling type', while another member of Harrison's battalion maintained that at least half the incidents described in the book never occurred.[1]

Relevance to contemporary readers

To many readers today, World War I must seem like ancient history. But the impact of this war on the rest of the twentieth century was immense. The seeds of World War II, the most destructive war in all of human history, were planted in World War I. The disarray in which Europe was left after World War I – especially the Treaty of Versailles, which heavily

[1] J Vance, *The Formulation of Historical Consciousness: a case study in literature*, University of British Columbia, 2001, p.5.

punished and further humiliated the defeated Germany – paved the way for the rise of Adolf Hitler's Nazi regime, whose outrageous conduct was instrumental in sparking off World War II. The effects of that war continue to be felt today.

World War I helped to shape future attitudes to war itself. The strong enthusiasm with which the participating countries greeted the coming of the war gradually dissipated as the horrendous nature of the slaughter became known. This became so terrible that it was deemed to be 'the war to end all wars' and, while that hope has clearly not been fulfilled, Western countries have never again marched so enthusiastically into war.

The fact that war persists as a feature of human life to the present day, however, adds to the relevance of this novel. It sometimes appears that every new generation needs to be reminded of the words of the American Civil War general William Tecumseh Sherman: 'I am sick and tired of war. Its glory is all moonshine ... War is hell'.[2] Just as war itself has been a common thread in human life down through the ages, so too has opposition to war. Fifty years after the outbreak of World War I, during the Vietnam War, Vietnamese Buddhist monk and poet Thich Nhat Hanh, in his poem 'Condemnation', spoke out 'to denounce this dreadful war,/ this murder of brothers by brothers!' He went on to ask: 'If we kill our brothers and sisters, what will we have left?/With whom shall we live?'[3]

Harrison's novel leads us to speculate about why humans continue to resort to war in response to international disputes, while being fully aware of its destructiveness. The questions posed by an American soldier in Vietnam – 'My God, what do we do to ourselves? Why do we hate ourselves so much that we have to kill each other?'[4] – are implicit also in *Generals Die in Bed*. If we compare the poetry of veterans of World War I with that of veterans of the Vietnam War, we find a common sense of outrage over being lied to by the political leaders who led – or misled – them into war. We find, too, a common sense of shock at the cruelty

---

[2] *Bloomsbury Thematic Dictionary of Quotations*, Bloomsbury, London, 1991, p.436.

[3] Thich Nhat Hanh, *Call Me By My True Names*, Parallax Press, Albany, California, 1999, p.39.

[4] Bernard Edelman, ed., *Dear America – letters home from Vietnam*, Norton, London, 2002 (first published 1985), p.198.

of war and the utter misery it causes to human beings. The literature of anti-war protest, given immense impetus by soldiers' responses to World War I, continues to this day. Shortly after the American invasion of Iraq in 2003, for example, an anthology entitled *101 Poems Against War* appeared throughout the English-speaking world.

Relevance to Australian readers

World War I is still a vital part of our national story. While our role in the war still tends to be associated with the landing at Gallipoli on 25 April 1915 and with the subsequent fighting there, the fact is that most of our many casualties from the war occurred in France. Of the nearly 60 000 Australians who died in battle, 48 000 died there. Streets named after the various battles on the French fields, such as Amiens, Passchendaele and Ypres, can be found in every state of Australia. Almost 65 per cent of all Australian soldiers in this war were either killed or wounded. Such a massive death toll from a country with such a small population greatly harmed the growing nation.

The political disputes that precipitated the war in Europe had nothing to do with Australia. Our involvement in the war can be seen as one link in a chain of Australian military involvements in the wars of other countries. But we need to remember that the Australia of 1914 was very different from the Australia of today. As a part of the British Empire, and as a country whose citizens were mostly of British descent, our ties to Britain were very strong. It was assumed that Australia would come to the assistance of the 'Mother Country'. The Prime Minister at the time of the outbreak of war, Andrew Fisher, declared that Australia would fight 'to the last man and the last shilling' in support of Britain. Young Australian men in their droves volunteered for overseas service, and those who did not were often sent white feathers, a symbol of cowardice, in the mail. The same occurred in Britain.

This was in the earlier months of the war. As the death toll began to rise alarmingly, voluntary enlistments began to diminish and the fanatically pro-war Prime Minister, William 'Billy' Hughes, sought to introduce conscription for overseas service. He held two referenda on the issue: each was narrowly defeated. The campaigns both for and against these referenda generated enormous bitterness and sectarian division. It was at this time that the then Roman Catholic Archbishop of Melbourne, Daniel Mannix, became known across Australia for his implacable opposition to conscription. The opposition of Catholics, as well as of soldiers at the front, helped to defeat the referenda.

The literature of World War I

The war gave birth to a vast literature, much of it a literature of protest. World War II, by contrast, generated far less literature. The awfulness of World War I appears to have shocked many soldiers into print; without doubt, they needed to unburden themselves of the horrors they had witnessed. *Generals Die in Bed* can be placed within this body of literature.

It would be particularly valuable to study *Generals Die in Bed* alongside the works on life in the trenches by Hemingway, Graves and Remarque that were published in 1929, and especially alongside some of the excellent poetry that emerged from the war. Indeed, the changing treatment of the subject in poetry as the war dragged on reflected the changing attitudes to it. The poetry of Rupert Brooke, for example, an Englishman who died of disease before ever taking part in a battle, reflects a view of war as glorious and heroic: a view that rapidly became obsolete. Brooke's poem, 'Peace', speaks of the violence of war as cleansing; he depicts soldiers going to the war as 'swimmers into cleanness leaping'.[5] It would be hard to find a more incongruous image than that one, and many of the poems that followed, especially those by Wilfred Owen and Siegfried Sassoon, are filled with images that shock the reader with their descriptions of the horrors of the war.

---

[5] IM Parsons, ed., *Men Who March Away: poems of the First World War*, The Hogarth Press, London, 1987, p.40.

Both Owen and Sassoon spent time as patients in Craiglockhart psychiatric hospital in 1917, and you may be interested to read a fictionalised account of their experiences in Pat Barker's *The Regeneration Trilogy*. A work such as *Generals Die in Bed* leads us to wonder about the psychological damage caused to veterans of the war, and Barker's trilogy of novels sheds much light on this.

The causes of the war

Many millions of words have been written and spoken about the build-up to World War I. My aim here is to give no more than a brief overview of this: there are countless books on the subject if you wish to read in greater detail.

The roots of the war can be traced to the formation of rival alliances between European nations in the years leading up to it. Hostility between France and Germany dated back to the Franco-Prussian War, which ended in 1871. The German Chancellor, Otto Von Bismarck, knowing that France wanted revenge for its defeat in the war, formed an alliance in 1879 with Austria-Hungary. This was known as the Dual Alliance. In 1882 Italy joined this alliance, although it was later to fight on the side of Britain and her allies during World War I. In 1894, France formed an alliance with Russia, in which Russia agreed to go to war with Germany if France were attacked by Germany, or by Germany and Italy combined, and France agreed to support Russia if it were attacked by Germany or by Germany and Austria. Meanwhile, tensions between Britain and Germany were building up. One of the first instances of this was the proposal by Germany to England that the two nations should divide between them the large Portuguese colonies of Angola and Mozambique. Britain rebuffed Germany, preferring Portuguese ownership to German, and Germany did not forgive the rebuff. When the British began to falter in their war against the Boers in South Africa (the Boer War of 1899–1902), for example, Germany publicly congratulated the Boer leader.

The importance of nationalism and militarism

At this point, it is worth commenting on the role of nationalism in triggering the war. A picture emerges of the Germany of this time as an aggressive, militaristic and nationalistic power on the European scene. Germany's militarism could be seen in its large-scale naval expansion after 1900. This made Britain nervous, as it was fearful that a powerful German navy could threaten its own navy, which had the task of defending the trade routes for Britain's worldwide empire.

Not that nationalism was a powerful force only in Germany: it was certainly powerful also in Britain and in the other belligerent countries. Its strength was clearly shown by the enthusiastic rush of young men to enlist in the military after the declaration of war. Britain was, indeed, still a principal world power, in possession of a vast empire and a very powerful navy. Washington had not yet replaced London as the centre of the Western world.

The formation of rival alliances

The Entente Cordiale (Cordial Understanding) of 1904: France and Great Britain

France, like Britain, was worried about Germany's naval expansion, and as a result those two countries decided to resolve whatever differences remained between them. They came to a cordial 'understanding' (entente), by which France agreed to surrender all claims to Egypt and recognise Britain's 'historic rights' there, in return for Britain's recognition of French interests in Morocco. While this was not a military alliance, it had the potential to pave the way for such an alliance if events proved it necessary.

The Triple Entente of 1907: France, Britain and Russia

With France and Britain, and France and Russia on good terms, steps were taken to remove remaining Anglo-Russian antagonism so that all three nations could work together for common interests. Once the sources of tension between Britain and Russia were removed, there was nothing to prevent France, Britain and Russia from forming an 'understanding' between themselves, and that understanding became known as the Triple Entente.

So, by 1907 six nations were aligned in two groups of three: the military, defensive alliance of Germany, Austria and Italy, and the diplomatic understanding of Britain, France and Russia. Two other facts were also certain: Germany was the greatest power in Europe and the British Empire was the greatest world power. Germany's political and military activities, coupled with tremendous economic growth, were making it a rival to Britain.

The Sarajevo crisis, June 1914

In June 1914 the Austrian archduke and his wife travelled to Bosnia to review two Austrian army corps stationed there. The ceremonies included a visit to Sarajevo, the capital city of the region. It was there that the Archduke and his wife were shot by an assassin, Gavrilo Princip.

The assassination *in itself* did not start the war, but it worsened tensions already existing between Austria and Serbia, and started a chain reaction in which the tensions between the rival alliances ultimately led to war. The murder provided Austria with the opportunity it needed to eliminate Serbia as a political power, because Austria feared that Serbian propaganda and agitation were a threat to the Austro-Hungarian Empire. There was some reason for this fear, as Serbia was the centre of a pan-Slav movement demanding that all Slavs in the Austrian Empire unite and become independent. The German kaiser (ruler) allowed himself to be convinced that Germany's interests were vitally concerned in this dispute, and he virtually gave Austria a 'blank cheque' to present an ultimatum to Serbia. The Serbian government responded favourably, and for a time the crisis appeared to have been defused.

However, a series of diplomatic blunders on the part of France and Russia on the one side and Germany and Austria on the other culminated in Austria's declaration of war on Serbia on 28 July 1914, even though Serbia had accepted almost all Austria's demands. Other European powers were sure that Germany was behind this, reasoning that Austria's rejection of Serbia's conciliatory reply to the ultimatum proved that Austria wanted to extend its influence in the Balkans, and that it would not have dared to act in this way without Germany's support. The next blunder was the Russian czar's (ruler's) agreement to general and full mobilisation of troops for war. On the afternoon of 31 July, Germany sent Russia a telegram stating that unless Russia stopped mobilising by 12 noon on 1 August, Germany would declare war. When no reply had come from Russia by 5 p.m., Germany declared war.

The rival alliance system begins to take effect

Germany understood that France would support Russia, and had long determined that if it were ever engaged in a two-front war with France and Russia it must attack France first, because France could mobilise faster than Russia. On 31 July, Germany asked France what action it would take if war broke out between Germany and Russia. On 1 August France replied that it would consult its own interests and immediately began to mobilise. On 3 August, Germany declared war on France.

On 31 July, Britain had asked both France and Germany whether they would respect Belgium's neutrality should they go to war with each other. France replied that it would, but Germany refused to answer. In fact, Germany had already decided that it would be much easier to advance through Belgium than to attack the forts on the French eastern frontier.

On 2 August, Germany occupied Luxembourg and then demanded that German troops be allowed to pass through Belgium. The Belgian king refused and so on 4 August, German troops crossed the frontier into Belgium, thereby violating that country's neutrality. Britain, greatly concerned at this German move, sent an ultimatum to Germany, insisting that it respect Belgium's neutrality. Germany replied that 'necessity knows no laws' and accused Britain of making war 'just for a scrap of paper' – that is, the guarantee of neutrality that Britain and other powers had given Belgium in 1839. On the same day, 4 August, Britain declared war on Germany. World War I had begun. 'The lamps are going out all over Europe' remarked Lord Grey, the British Foreign Secretary, 'and we will not see them lit again in our lifetime'.[6] His words proved prophetic.

The nature of the war on the Western front

All the Great Powers were confident that they could achieve a relatively rapid victory in the war. Young men on both sides rushed to enlist, believing that the war would be over by Christmas. Few people anticipated the bruising stalemate into which the war settled for much of the next four years. After the initial rapid German advance into France, the war bogged down in that country as the rival combatants became literally entrenched – digging themselves into opposing trenches which faced each other across the barren wasteland that became known as 'No Man's Land'. Eventually, the trench system stretched from the Swiss border to the English Channel.

The defensive capacities of the rival armies were so great that neither side could break the stalemate. Attempts to do so, and thus restore the war of movement, failed as both sides threw huge numbers of troops up against each other, resulting in mass slaughter. On 1 July 1916, for example, the first day of the Battle of the Somme, the British army suffered approximately 57 000 casualties, 20 000 of them fatalities. The devastating effects of the machine gun had never previously been seen. The dominant image of warfare was still one of cavalry charges and a strategy whereby, in the words of the American general William Prescott, soldiers would not fire 'until [they] saw the whites of [the enemy's] eyes'. As the battle continued between 2 July and mid-September, British guns fired over seven million shells into the German positions on the River Somme. The battle became known as the *'materialschlact'* – the munitions offensive.[7]

The United States' entry into the war in April 1917, which brought with it fresh troops and superior weaponry, finally began to break the deadlock and restore the war of movement. On 8 August 1918, the British, the

[6] Barry Jones, *Decades of Decision, 1860–*, Horwitz Publications, Sydney, 1965, p.154.

[7] Robin Prior & Trevor Wilson, *The First World War*, Cassell, London, 2001, p.135.

Canadians and the Australians broke the German morale – but not their lines – at Amiens, and this was followed by rapid American and French advances in the south. This is the battle in which the narrator of *Generals Die in Bed* is wounded. An armistice was finally signed on 11 November 1918, at 11 a.m. This date is still observed as Armistice Day (more widely known as Remembrance Day) throughout the Western world.

Life in the trenches

Harrison provides a detailed picture of conditions in the trenches, as do other soldier-writers on both sides of the conflict. The plagues of rats and lice are frequently described, as is the constant danger from enemy snipers. Many soldiers died from sniper fire on their first day in the trenches. It has been estimated that up to a third of Allied casualties on the Western Front were sustained in them. An additional menace was mustard gas, which sank down into the trenches, forcing the inhabitants out and exposing them to enemy fire.

Canada in World War I

As a country belonging, like Australia, to the British Empire, Canada entered the war in 1914 and its troops served for the duration.[8] By 1916 the Canadians had formed four divisions, with a fifth to provide reinforcements. The four divisions of the Canada Corps earned an outstanding reputation as a fighting force. Canada's participation in the war, like Australia's, showed that it was playing an important role in world affairs and this helped to undo both countries' colonial status. Before the war ended in 1918, more than 619 000 Canadian officers and men had enlisted, including some 22 000 who had served in the British Royal Air Force. More than 60 000 Canadians were killed in action or died of wounds – like the Australian death toll, a high number in relation to the total population.

[8] Further information about Canada's participation in World War I may be found at http://www.thecanadianencyclopedia.ca/en/article/first-world-war-wwi/

The cost of the war

It is impossible to measure the total cost of this war. While statistics cannot convey the horrors of the war, they can give some idea of the scale of the suffering:

- 65 million people were directly involved
- 9 million were killed or died of wounds
- 22 million were wounded
- 5 million were missing in action – many bodies were simply obliterated
- 9 million civilians died of starvation, epidemics and massacres
- 30 million died in total, twice the losses of all the wars of the nineteenth century.

The Carnegie Institute estimated the cost of the war at $400 billion – enough to provide every family in Britain, Belgium, Russia, the US, Germany, Canada and Australia with a house worth $4000 (including land and furniture), create library and university facilities worth $15 million in most cities of 20 000 or more, and double the pay of the world's teachers and nurses.[9]

The war marked the turning point of the twentieth century, for much of the history of the modern world hinges on the events of those four years. The war ended four great empires – Russia, Germany, Turkey and Austria-Hungary – and destroyed the remnants of absolute monarchy. The Bolshevik Revolution in the Soviet Union (ushering in the Communist state), the Weimar Republic (which became Adolf Hitler's Third Reich in 1933) and Kemal Atatürk's Turkish republic were all by-products of the war.

[9] Barry Jones, *Decades of Decision, 1860–*, p.167.

GENRE, STYLE & STRUCTURE

Genre

It is difficult to classify neatly a work such as *Generals Die in Bed*. The two main forms of prose in response to war in the twentieth century have been quite similar in nature. The first is personal memoir (such as *Goodbye to All That*); the second is the autobiographically based novel (such as *A Farewell to Arms*). Harrison's work appears closer to the first kind of text: while his narrator is anonymous, it is clear that much of the substance of the book is drawn directly from his personal experience in the trenches of Europe. Harrison traces the experiences of his narrator from his departure for the war to his wounding at the Battle of Amiens and his subsequent repatriation. Perhaps the narrator's anonymity is meant to convey the impression that he could have been one of any number of combatants, to suggest that his experiences were far from uncommon and that many thousands shared similar sufferings.

It would be wrong to assume that the book is anything like a police court record of what Harrison witnessed. It is possible to argue, as does the writer Wright Morris, that 'anything processed by memory is fiction'.[10] The subjective element of such memoirs is indeed strong, and this is especially true of Harrison's, since he clearly set out to deliver a strongly anti-war message by highlighting the worst aspects of the war and particular attitudes to it. Harrison's purpose is not to write a history of the war, but rather to register his protest against it. His characters all die in hideous ways. Although the scene in which the narrator bayonets Karl, the German, is credible, it is almost certainly a fictional episode to underline the tragedy of war, and the scenes in London are constructed to condemn the English public's attitude towards the war. Wilfred Owen described the subject of his poetry as 'the pity of war' and this, too, is Harrison's subject. We do not have to look very deeply into the text to see

---

[10] Paul Fussell, *The Great War and Modern Memory*, Oxford University Press, London, 1977, p.205.

that he intends to convey this sense of the pity of war, as well as a sense of anger that so many young lives were wasted in it.

If we consider *Generals* as a work of fiction (as the publishers of the book have done), then this raises the question: can we categorise it as a novel? It has aspects of that type of novel which describes in episodic fashion the adventures of a young man who sets forth on a coming-of-age experience. Yet the book lacks the detailed development of character and the creative element that typify most novels. Harrison's style is much closer to journalism than to a novel.

We could also describe a work like *Generals* as a therapeutic work. By this, I mean it is a work composed by its author as a means of relieving himself of the burdens of traumatic memories, in the manner of many other soldier-writers of this and other wars. By recording their memories, such writers objectify them and thereby seek to reduce the hold that such memories have over their lives. The Vietnam War veteran and writer, Tim O'Brien, for example, wrote of telling his stories in order 'to relieve at least some of the pressure on my dreams'.[11] And there is plenty of the stuff of bad dreams in *Generals Die in Bed.*

Finally, Harrison's text belongs to the genre of the memorialising text. That is, it sets out to do in words what the war memorial does in stone – to ensure that the sacrifices and sufferings of so many will never be forgotten. Harrison's dedication 'to the bewildered youths' of Britain, Australia, Canada and Germany who were killed near Amiens on the day he was wounded makes this clear. So does the remark of the narrator to Gladys that the English civilians who are trying to forget the war 'should be made to remember' (p.125).

Style

As befitting the subject, Harrison's prose has a tough, pared-down quality that emphasises the physical reality of the war. He tends to use rougher, blunter Germanic and older English words rather than the smoother,

[11] Tim O'Brien, *The Things They Carried*, Collins, London, 1990, p.43.

longer Latinate words. He creates images which he places before us like snapshots from a slide-show – his is a highly visual style which enables us to see in our mind's eye what he is describing. The use of detail is telling: Harrison has an eye for the shocking, sometimes poignant detail.

A prominent feature of the writing is the shortness of the paragraphs – often, a paragraph is no longer than one short sentence. This style creates a sense of dislocation. It suggests that the soldier's life is lived from moment to moment as he struggles merely to survive from one minute to the next. It is a style that reflects uncertainty, tension and a lack of belief in any coherent future – or in any kind of future at all.

The story is told in the present tense. This adds a sense of immediacy and directness: the narrator is embroiled in the events he describes, rather than being distanced from them. At times, the narrative reads like an internal monologue, or a series of diary entries from the narrator.

Structure

Harrison's story is told chronologically, from his departure from Montreal to his wounding at Amiens, with his experiences in the war zone and on leave in London forming the bulk of the narrative. It is a fairly formulaic narrative structure, in which the narrator leaves his homeland for a foreign war, becomes deeply shocked and disillusioned and returns home, irrevocably changed. His story is structured around the pattern familiar to the soldiers of a battalion: a spell in the frontline, followed by a stint in support, then in reserve lines and then a period of rest before the cycle begins again.

CHAPTER-BY-CHAPTER ANALYSIS

Chapter 1: 'Recruits' (pp.11–17)

Summary: *The narrator, newly recruited to the army, leaves Montreal for the war.*

The narrative begins in the matter-of-fact style that characterises it throughout, in a barracks bunk room in Montreal. The opening scene is squalid – indeed, this is one of the words used to describe the houses in the area of Montreal where the action begins. The lights shining from these houses, however, shine with 'an inviting, warm glow' (p.11). They contrast with the few 'jaundiced' (p.11) electric lights burning in the bunk room, the word 'jaundiced' carrying an association with illness. This contrast is prophetic: it foreshadows the environment into which the soldiers in the barracks will soon be cast – a harsh, ugly world far removed from ordinary domestic comforts.

The first character introduced is Anderson, who from the outset is defined in terms of his fundamentalist religious convictions. A Methodist lay preacher (a person who is sometimes called upon to preach the sermon in church although not ordained), he is openly critical of what he sees as immoral behaviour by the other men. Commenting on their recent visits to local prostitutes, he asserts that: 'Some of you men would put your bodies where I wouldn't put my swagger stick' (p.14). There is a dark though unintentional irony when he further contends: 'Well, anyway, God didn't make your bodies for *that*' (p.14). Reading these words again after reading the entire narrative, we may reflect that God didn't make their bodies to be destroyed in war, either.

The war song sung by some of the soldiers in their drunken state is another ominous sign of things to come – the laments, 'I'm too young to die' and 'I want to go home' (p.13) stand in stark contrast to other songs of the war, such as the incongruously cheery, 'We don't want to lose you, but we think you ought to go/For your King and Country both need you so'.

More than half of the battalion leaves for war drunk – perhaps this is really the only state in which they can cope with such a departure. By this stage of the war – 1916 appears to be the year, although it is never directly stated – the soldiers would have had some idea of what they were getting into. There is certainly no bravado or enthusiasm on the part of the men. Of more interest is the reaction of the women who farewell the soldiers – they are 'hysterical' (p.16) – and we can speculate over the reason for this. Are they excited by the sight of soldiers in uniform leaving for war? Are they unaware of the reality of what the soldiers are going into, or are they in denial? Are they perhaps disturbed by their departure? Whatever the truth, the women are strongly aroused by the soldiers – it is an emotional scene – and the perfumed woman who throws herself upon the narrator gives him his last taste of sensual pleasure for a long time. She embodies softness and solace; the word 'soft' (p.16) is used three times to describe her. In contrast to this softness, the narrator conveys a sense of harshness and heaviness: the heaviness of his reluctant heart as he sets off for war, of his boots and 'leaden' pack (p.17). His mood is troubled: from the sickly yellow or 'jaundiced' lights of the barracks, the men set off 'green' and 'white-faced' (p.17).

Q How would you explain the behaviour of the women farewelling the troops?

Q How effective do you find this chapter as an opening to the story?

Chapter 2: 'In the trenches' (pp.19–31)

Summary: *The narrator experiences the dangers and discomforts of trench warfare.*

Without any intervening explanation – like a rapid cut from one scene to another in a movie – the narrator moves the action to the war itself, to Belgium and the 'rubble that was once a little ... peasant town' (p.19). The earth itself has been scarred by the war, just like the men, who tear their hands and clothes on the 'barbed wire that runs through the earth as though it were a geological deposit' (p.19). This jarring image is a metaphor for the nature of the war zone itself. It powerfully highlights the destructiveness of war. For the first time, the narrator emphasises the immense discomfort of life in the trenches. The language focuses on the ubiquitous impediments to natural ease of movement: Fry 'slither[s] into a water-filled hole' (p.19); the oncoming men 'stumble' on others and 'trip over' them (p.20).

At this point, Clark, the captain, an 'Imperial ... Englishman', is briefly introduced (p.20). He is the first military authority figure in the narrative, and the impression we are given of him is immediately unfavourable: he 'glories in his authority' (p.20), showing little sympathy for the men under his command. This is the first sign of the narrator's highly negative view of those in military authority.

At midnight, the narrator and his friend, Fry, keep watch on sentry duty. In the silence, the men engage in desultory conversation. The narrator tries to imagine Montreal, but his 'images are murky' (p.23): in this strange, alien environment, it has not taken long for memories of his homeland to fade. His mind fills instead with nightmarish images of his comrades dead: 'They are stiff and ... white and set in the stillness of death' (p.24). A 'rat ... as large as a tomcat' (p.24) leaps towards him, adding to his distress.

At this point, the stillness of the night is suddenly shattered as '*minenwerfer*' (p.25) – mine-throwing trench mortars – are launched from the German positions. The narrator depicts what follows as if he is actually reliving it, describing the effects of the explosions from moment to moment, as if each may be his last. The emphasis is on the physical symptoms of his fear – 'My bowels liquefy' (p.26) – but especially on the terrible, overpowering noise. Fry is 'whimpering' (p.26); 'The air screams and howls'; the bombardment 'screams and rages and boils like an angry sea' (p.27). The blunt, monosyllabic words 'scream', 'shriek', 'howl' and 'roar' are aptly chosen; they all connote perturbation and distress. In the midst of this mayhem, the narrator sees the 'stars shining serenely above us' (p.27), the only sign of sanity in this man-made hell. But those stars are quite indifferent to the hell unfolding beneath them and the narrator feels a sense of terrible isolation and disorientation in the midst of it: there is no solid ground, whether literal or metaphorical, for him. His cries to God lead him to remember that he does not, after all, believe in God, and that he has no explanation for 'this mad fury, this maniacal congealed hatred that pours down on our heads' (p.27). The only small scraps of comfort he can find come from nature, from the earth around him: from the piece of mud that flies into his mouth, 'cool and refreshing', and from the 'cool, damp earth' in which he buries his head (p.28).

The list of the soldiers' enemies lengthens. It is not just the Germans who threaten their wellbeing, but also the rats and the lice that breed in their filthy uniforms and drive them mad with itching. Meanwhile, the narrator finds a boot containing a severed foot, which leads him to recall seeing Brown's foot, the heel of which is 'as raw as a lump of meat' (p.31).

Q Examine the ways in which the author contrasts the human world with the natural world in this chapter.

Q How does this chapter illustrate the rapid dehumanisation of the soldiers?

Chapter 3: 'Out on rest' (pp.33–43)

Summary: *A brief respite from fighting.*

On 'rest' from the trenches in a peasant village, the narrator digresses briefly about how military terms such as this one often mean 'something altogether different' (p.34). 'Rest' for the soldiers means endless marching, followed by a short period of real rest, followed by 'an interminable routine of fatigues' (p.34), or military tasks – this term, at least, seems to be aptly named. Another military misnomer is an 'artillery duel'. The term 'duel' has connotations of an old-fashioned, carefully stage-managed contest between two feuding individuals, or even a fencing contest. In reality, it is a sudden, terrifying and lethal battle between the competing armies. It is interesting to note that the reluctance of the military to call things by their true names continues today, with its use of euphemisms such as 'friendly fire' or 'collateral damage'.

This chapter is also noteworthy for the light it sheds on two characters: Clark, the captain, and Brown. The narrator's negative depiction of his captain continues: he is clearly a vain man, one who 'takes an insufferable pride in his uniform'; even 'his equipment and insignia gleam malignantly' (p.34). His lectures on cleanliness (a way of boosting morale) appear quite absurd in the context of the war.

Key point

The narrator's resentment of Clark is typical of the resentment he feels against the whole officer class – a group of men with special rights and privileges who show little empathy for the men serving under them.

Brown often seems to come 'under Clark's displeasure' (p.35), as well as that of the sergeant, Johnson (p.41). He appears to be accident-prone, and as such, he is often used as a scapegoat when things go wrong. Here he ends up with 'two hours pack drill' (p.41), a punishment which seems tedious, painful and pointless. The news of Brown's punishment leads to Fry's tirade against the officers who inflict such misery: 'They take everything from us: our lives, our blood, our hearts; even the few lousy hours of rest, they take those, too. Our job is to give, and theirs is to take' (p.43).

It is not surprising, then, that the men see some of their officers as a greater enemy than the Germans themselves. They never refer to the Germans as their enemy, and would never describe them in the language of newspaper writers back home, who demonise them with the word 'Hun'. Here, as so often in this work, the view of the war held by those actually fighting it is set in stark contrast with that of those at home. The soldiers 'have learned who [their] enemies are – the lice, some of [their] officers, and Death' (p.39). Significantly, the narrator capitalises that last word: Death is the ultimate enemy in what has become a struggle for mere survival.

Q How does the author establish the nature of the relationship between the officers and the men serving under them?

Q What aspects of the narrator's character are starting to emerge?

Chapter 4: 'Back to the round' (pp.45–53)

Summary: *Back in the frontline trenches; Brown is shot dead by a sniper.*

The dreary round continues: six days in reserve, six in support, six in the front trenches, then rest. The sense of monotony is reinforced by the repeated use of the word 'same'. The rats and the lice are the only creatures to thrive: this environment is plainly unsuitable for humans. Indeed, all nature seems blighted by the war; the trees, too, 'are skeletons holding stubs of stark, shell-amputated arms towards the sky' (pp.45–6). '[T]he odours of the trenches rise in a miasmal mist' (p.46) – a miasma is a suffocating, oxygen-starved vapour. The image reinforces the sense of an environment unfit for human habitation. Once again, the narrator reminds us that the officer who gave instruction in trench warfare is safe and comfortable at the base, far from the realities of the trenches. The training given by such men has turned the frontline soldiers into 'will-less robots' (p.47). Almost certainly, though, this is the only state in which the men could carry on.

Outside the trenches, snipers are a constant threat, and the unfortunate Brown becomes a victim. The men divide up his rations, reasoning, 'Anyway ... he can't eat any more' (p.53). Interestingly, the narrator's attitude towards the sniper is not hostile. In sadly prophetic words, the narrator imagines himself and his comrades 'fall[ing] upon him and bayonet[ing] him like a hapless trench rat' (p.48). His pleading utterance of the word '*comrade*', that 'beautiful word ... born in suffering and sorrow' (p.48), will be of no avail, laments the narrator. Here is evidence of the humanitarian values that the narrator holds, but which his participation in the war prevents him from putting into practice.

Q Why do you think the account of Brown's death is introduced at this stage of the narrative?

Q How is the narrator's growing opposition to the war revealed in this chapter?

Chapter 5: 'On rest again' (pp.55–71)

Summary: *An unexpected attack, followed by rest, a swim and conversation.*

While on their way to rest, the men once again come under fire. This time, it is the unfortunate horses who suffer, 'Their eyes ... distended like those of frightened women' (p.56), their noises terrible. The terror past, the men lie prostrate in a field and find a moment of relief at last. 'The air is filled with the heavy fragrance' of the 'blossoming beans' in a nearby field (p.59).

Key point

In this image, the narrator shows us the beauty, stillness and sanity of nature, a profound contrast to the madness of the war; a small, delicious taste of the way things ought to be.

Later in the chapter, the narrator describes a similar moment, when some of the men swim naked in a stream a few kilometres from the village in which they are billeted (p.68). Underneath their uniforms, the men have the bodies of boys: 'slim, hard, graceful bodies' (p.68), deserving to be put to uses other than war. Relieved of their uniforms, they feel an 'animal pleasure', 'a feeling of security, of deep inward happiness' (p.69). This, again, is the way things ought to be. It represents what the American poet Denise Levertov described as 'the quickness, the sureness,/the deep intelligence living at peace would have'.[12]

It is interesting to note that scenes of soldiers bathing are included in many memoirs of the war. In his classic work *The Great War and Modern Memory*, Paul Fussell remarks:

> Watching men (usually 'one's own men') bathing naked becomes a set-piece scene in almost every memory of the war. And this conventional vignette of soldiers bathing under

[12] Hayden Carruth, ed., *The Voice that is Great Within Us – American poetry of the twentieth century*, Bantam Books, New York, 1970, p.516.

> the affectionate eye of their young officers recurs not because soldiers bathe but because there's hardly a better way of projecting poignantly the awful vulnerability of mere naked flesh. The quasi-erotic and the pathetic conjoin in these scenes to emphasize the stark contrast between beautiful frail flesh and the alien metal that waits to violate it.[13]

Such images have proved persistent. In Bill Couturie's 1988 documentary of the Vietnam War, *Dear America,* for example, footage of American soldiers swimming in the South China Sea are juxtaposed with footage of heavy guns blasting from a helicopter. Similarly, in Harrison's novel, the narrator reminds us that the soldiers' delight in the water will soon be forgotten when 'the rumble of the guns' (p.69) in the distance makes its presence felt. This background noise persists like 'the subdued throbbing of violins' (p.70), an image associated with both pain and melancholy. Towards the end of the chapter there are other poignant images: the local village lads who 'have the faces of little old men' (p.69) – clearly, all the civilians of the village have been suffering – and the ominous image of the dead Frenchman, whose body floats down the river from the battlefields of the Somme. This image embodies the potential fate of all the men.

In the midst of their various activities, the men converse among themselves and their conversation tells of their concerns. They reflect on Brown's death – he has now become a 'symbol' (p.60) of the many, many war dead, a symbol, too, of what may happen to each of them. His widow has also become a symbol of all the bereaved wives of dead soldiers. They share scraps of rumour, the most alarming being that they are going to be 'fatten[ed] ... up' in preparation for a 'big scrap' (p.62). The old cliché 'lambs to the slaughter' seems most appropriate here.

Q Explore the author's use of contrasts in this chapter.

Q Does the second half of this chapter prepare us for what follows in the next?

---

[13] Paul Fussell, *The Great War and Modern Memory*, p.299.

Chapter 6: 'Bombardment' (pp.73–104)

Summary: *The narrator volunteers for a raid on the German trenches; he kills a soldier, Karl, and takes Karl's brother and another German soldier prisoner.*

In this long chapter, the narrator records the full savagery of the war. A key theme of the chapter is the way in which war brutalises and dehumanises men, reducing them to the level of Stone Age barbarism. The men do not fight only the enemy; with nerves worn down by intolerable stress and chronic sleeplessness, they fight each other. It is a dog-eat-dog world, as Cleary and Broadbent are reduced to the level of animals, fighting over pieces of bread (p.74). This opening scene of the chapter shows that civilisation is a thin veneer, easily stripped away when circumstances are harsh enough.

The narrative once again settles down into a succession of clipped, broken, one-sentence paragraphs, each one re-creating the sense of struggle merely to get from one moment to the next. This struggle intensifies with the enemy bombardment. There is a sense of nothing less than cosmic disorder, as if 'an insane god is pounding [the trench] with Cyclopean fists, madly, incessantly' (p.77). The men sit as if they are 'prehistoric' (p.77). Their flickering candle is snuffed out, leaving them in literal and metaphorical darkness. It is not just the noise that disturbs; it is also the 'grotesque, fluttering shadows' (p.78) in the darkness, the stuff of nightmares long after the battle is over.

At this point Anderson prays, trying to ensure his survival, complaining that God will remove his favours if the men's swearing continues. The narrator is unimpressed, declaring: 'To think we could propitiate a senseless god by abstaining from cursing!' (p.80). Anderson's prayers bring to the narrator's mind the civilians back home praying for victory in the war – 'and that means', he concludes, 'that we must lie here and rot and tremble forever' (p.81). He feels contempt for the 'pallid preachers' (p.80) and their gods of fire and brimstone: no god could create a hell as terrible as the one through which he is living.

The brigade raid and the killing of Karl

There is a call for volunteers for a 'brigade' raid – an assault on the enemy trenches – for which the narrator volunteers. Now follows one of the most memorable and painful incidents of the book, in which the narrator bayonets to death a young German in his trench. This killing is described as if it is murder and later on, the narrator implies that it is such. During the killing, the narrator feels as if he has 'become insane'; he 'want[s] to strike again and again' (p.88). It must be the tension, the adrenaline rush caused by the primal instinct for survival, that makes him feel this way. That the killing occurs at such close quarters makes it particularly awful. This killing is personalised; the narrator and the German are brought together to 'enact our tragedy' (p.90). The obscenity of all war is telescoped down into this one incident. It is indeed a tragedy that in war men are forced to kill other men whom they do not even know well enough to hate. Little by little, the narrator humanises his enemy: he has a 'boyish face' with 'white down against green cheeks' (p.91).

The next Germans whom the narrator encounters and takes prisoner are also very young – 'boys of about seventeen' (p.92). They are really too young to be serving in the military at all, let alone in such a terrible place: 'Their uniforms are too big for them and their thin necks poke up out of enormous collars' (p.92), highlighting their tender years and inexperience. Neither of them has any more enthusiasm for the war than their enemies: '*Ach, es ist schrecklich – schrecklich*' ('Ah, it is terrible – terrible'), says one (p.96).

One of the prisoners identifies the comrade who has just been slain as his brother. We soon find out that his name was Karl, a naming that further humanises him. He is not just a faceless German; he is a brother and a son. Karl's brother is grateful to the narrator for his clemency: '*Du bist ein gutter Soldat*' ('You are a good soldier', p.96), he tells him. The narrator imagines Karl's mother writing to him, asking him to look after his younger brother. He wishes he could tell the surviving brother 'that something took us both, his brother and me, and dumped us into a lonely, shrieking hole at night – it armed us with deadly weapons and threw us against each other' (p.95). What was that 'something'?

Key point

We need not take this incident as a literal representation of one of the author's war experiences. More likely, it is a didactic fable – in this case, a story created to teach the reader something of the tragedy of war, and to highlight the humanitarian values that the narrator holds, which war so often destroys. The details of the story support this interpretation: the emphasis on the shared humanity of the combatants, which survives beyond the brutality; the word *'Kamarad'* (comrade) used by the Germans to address their enemy in battle; the dressing of the wounded German's wounds; the sharing of cigarettes; the sadness expressed on both sides over the killing.

In terms of its essential purpose – to show the pity and tragedy of war – this incident can be compared to similar moments depicted in the literature of war. One that comes to mind from World War I poetry is found in Wilfred Owen's poem, 'Strange Meeting'.[14] This poem relates an imaginary meeting between two soldiers, one English, the other the German he has killed. In the last stanza of the poem, the dead German declares, in a seemingly paradoxical statement that encapsulates the absurdity of war: 'I am the enemy you killed, my friend'. Similarly, in a story that takes its inspiration from the Vietnam War, 'The Man I Killed', Tim O'Brien creates a scene in which a young American soldier stands staring at the body of a Viet Cong soldier he has killed and he humanises his former enemy by imagining the details of his life.[15]

Now the narrator describes the aftermath of the raid. There is talk that the narrator will be awarded a military medal, but he feels little satisfaction in this and he refuses the offer of the prisoner's cap that a captain from another company tells him to send to his mother as a 'souvenir' (p.98). The narrator's initial emotions are a sense of relief that the raid is over, sorrow at the loss of more than forty men in the fighting and a sense of pride that he has 'been tested and found not wanting' (p.98).

Soon afterwards, the narrator begins to break down, as the strain of what he has endured begins to be released. His emotions take control: 'I

[14] Wilfred Owen, *The Collected Poems of Wilfred Owen*, ed. C Day Lewis, Chatto & Windus, London, 1963, p.35.
[15] Tim O'Brien, *The Things They Carried*, Collins, London, 1990.

do not think things now; I feel them' (p.99). He is haunted by the image of Karl, dead on the end of his bayonet. This is a classic case of a person coping with the stress of an event while it is occurring, but not coping with the aftermath. Action has provided a release for the narrator, but now he is left to contemplate the results of that action. It pays not to think too much when you are a soldier in combat. The narrator recalls the comment by one of his sergeants, that 'a strong back and a weak mind' (p.103) are all that a soldier needs.

The chapter ends with an account of the death of Cleary, which reminds the narrator of the many deaths he has witnessed in the war. He rails against the men who have 'stolen' (p.104) his life and the lives of his comrades. 'Back home', he reflects, 'we were factors in what we were doing' (p.104). But in the war zone, 'we are no more factors than was the stripling Isaac whom the hoary, senile Abraham led to the sacrificial block' (p.104). Here the narrator refers to the biblical story in which Abraham is prepared to sacrifice his son, Isaac, as an offering to God – a story that has often been the subject of Western art and literature. The narrator's anger is registered plainly through the contrast between the 'stripling' – a word that emphasises the boy's youth and vulnerability – and his 'hoary, senile' father. As is so often said, it is the old men who send the young out to die.

It is interesting to compare the author's reference to this story with that by Wilfred Owen in his poem, 'The Parable of the Old Man and the Young', with which Harrison would almost certainly have been familiar. Owen bases his poem upon the same biblical legend and concludes by describing the old man who 'slew his son,/And half the seed of Europe, one by one'.[16]

Q Examine what this chapter reveals about the dehumanising effects of war.

Q How would you respond to the sergeant's remark that 'all a soldier needed was a strong back and a weak mind' (p.103)?

---

[16] Wilfred Owen, *The Collected Poems*, p.42.

Chapter 7: Béthune (pp.107–19)

Summary: *The narrator spends a rest period in Béthune, enjoying simple pleasures.*

This is a chapter composed of a number of vignettes in which the narrator describes his brief respite from the war in the 'dirty, squat, coal-smudged' northern French city of Béthune (p.107). The people, like the civilians everywhere, appear miserable and downtrodden; they walk 'with that peculiar stunted walk of human moles' (pp.107–8). Though unattractive, the town is a 'haven' (p.108) for the Canadians: one has the impression that anywhere outside the trenches would be. Life for them is truly lived for the moment, for '[t]omorrow we may be dead' (p.110).

The narrator's contempt for military officers is again on display here. The general who arrives to inspect the men is 'A little grey-haired man' whose 'uniform is bedecked with gold and red facings' (p.111). Plainly, he spends most of his time cosseted in a rear-echelon position; he will 'never die in a lousy trench' because, as one of the men quips, 'Generals die in bed' (p.112). When Anderson asks, 'Where would we be without generals' (p.113) – which he intends as a rhetorical question – it is clear that the narrator and the rest of the men would give a very different answer from the one intended.

A scene of brief domestic comfort and simple sharing follows. This is another scene that serves to highlight normal, everyday pleasures of which the war has deprived the soldiers. The aroma of the narrator's pipe tobacco attracts the attention of an old peasant outside his cottage: tobacco is shared as the two men smoke and talk together and then the old man ushers the narrator into a bedroom, where he shares the bed with the man's daughter.

Passing an encampment of German prisoners of war, the Canadians throw them cigarettes and cans of bully beef. Clearly, it is not these men who are seen as the real enemy. The basic humanity of the Canadians finds expression in this brief scene.

Q What answer would the narrator give to the question 'Where would we be without generals' (p.113)?

Q Find the words to some of the songs of World War I.

Chapter 8: 'London' (pp.121–35)

Summary: *The narrator meets and stays with Gladys in London; the idealised notions of war held by the English civilians are shown to be naive and ignorant.*

Gladys

On leave in London, his reward for volunteering for the brigade raid, the narrator checks into a hotel, sleeps long and savours the solitude of which he has for so long been deprived. In a restaurant, he meets Gladys, clearly a friend to the soldiers, for she has 'enough for you all, poor lads' (p.124). She becomes 'that delightful combination of wife, mother, and courtesan' (p.130) for the narrator, attending to the full range of his needs. She is a nurturing, understanding woman who has plenty of experience in caring for other soldiers on leave from the front and she seems to know instinctively what to do. The narrator even confesses to her about his killing of Karl, describing his act as 'murder' (p.131). When she learns about the circumstances of the killing she is immediately reassured, but we can tell that the narrator is not, for he still considers his act to be murder. His reaction raises the question: is the distinction between murder and the state-sanctioned killing in war really valid?

Both Gladys and the narrator shed tears: both have good reasons to do so. If the narrator's tears spring from the relief and comfort of at last experiencing some love, Gladys' tears appear to spring from sadness at the thought of her lover returning to the hell from which he has temporarily escaped.

The ignorance of the civilians

The main theme of this chapter is the obvious ignorance and lack of awareness of what is happening in the war on the part of those at home in

England. One is reluctant to use the term, 'the home front', as that implies that the civilians are in some measure at least sharing in the sacrifices of a nation at war. Rather, life seems to be going on relatively undisturbed for those lucky enough to be out of the firing line. Two vignettes reveal this. The first is the scene at the theatre that the narrator attends with Gladys. It is a music hall performance, in which the war is depicted as a comical event by 'lewd female Tommies' whose 'breasts bob up and down' while singing 'Oh, it's a lovely war' (p.124). The inappropriateness of this is almost obscene. The narrator is enraged at it, and at the amused reactions of the civilians: 'I cannot formulate my hatred of these people' (p.126). These people are described with contempt. They live in a quite different world from the world of the war, and the narrator contrasts those two worlds with his usual eye for the telling physical detail: 'They sit here in stiff shirts, their faces and jowls are smooth with daily shaving and dainty cosmetics, their bellies are full, and out there we are being eaten by lice, we are sitting trembling in shivering dugouts' (p.126).

The second vignette is the narrator's account of his visit to Westminster Abbey and his meeting with an Anglican priest there. There is little doubt that the author has included this incident in the narrative in order to deepen his indictment of the civilians over their attitude to the war. Specifically, the attack here is on those representatives of the Christian clergy who used their influence and their pulpits to speak in favour of the war. The clergyman whom the narrator meets is one of these, 'known as a fighting parson' (p.133). It is easy for him to speak so enthusiastically in favour of the war for, as a clergyman, he is exempted from service.

Key point

It is incongruous that, as the representative of a religion advocating human brotherhood and nonviolence, the Anglican curate should be so enthusiastic about this war. Incongruous, too, is his assertion that the war 'has brought out the most heroic qualities in the common people, positively noble qualities' (p.134): an assertion that sits uneasily alongside the reality of what we have learnt from the narrative.

Q Write a monologue in which Gladys expresses her thoughts and feelings about the time she spends with the narrator.

Q Both Gladys and the narrator shed tears. How would you explain this?

Chapter 9: 'Over the top' (pp.137–56)

Summary: *Back on the frontline; Renaud dies horribly; Fry shoots Clark and then is killed as they retreat under fire.*

This is one of the most disturbing chapters of the book. Back at the front, the men wait in terrible suspense, beset by rumours about what is in store for them. A new offensive has been planned and the men are sent into the thick of it. The battle zone becomes literally a shambles – a slaughterhouse – with body parts everywhere. The Germans stage a human wave attack: it turns out that they have been drugged in preparation for this. The narrator, this time, feels a 'frenzied hatred' (p.148) for them; after all, they are setting out to kill him and in order to survive, he and his comrades become 'snarling, savage beasts' (p.148). In the midst of the mayhem, certain incidents stand out: Renaud's fear and his horrible death (p.153) and the slaying of a middle-aged German, whose cries that he is the father of three are to no avail (p.145).

Another notable incident in this chapter is the killing of the unpopular officer Clark by Fry, one of his own men. This incident underscores our sense of the hostility many soldiers felt towards their officers. We cannot be sure how many such incidents took place during the war, but we do know that, as the war grew increasingly unpopular with the troops, military discipline began to unravel. Significant mutinies took place in both the Russian and the French armies. In 1917, at least 150 000 French troops were court-martialled after they mutinied in protest at the tactics of the egregious General Nivelle, whose tactics resulted in 100 000 casualties in April of that year.

Q How are we positioned to respond to Clark's death and the manner of it?

Q What other signs are there that the soldiers' morale and discipline are beginning to unravel?

Chapter 10: 'An interlude' (pp.159–62)

Summary: *The narrator and Broadbent stay with a French family; they are promoted to corporal and sergeant respectively.*

This brief, aptly titled chapter sees the narrator and his comrade, Broadbent, billeted 'in a real house' (p.159), cared for by an elderly, motherly woman, who bathes the narrator's mutilated foot. This woman has two sons in the war; a fact that would explain her compassion towards the narrator, whom she treats as a surrogate son. The scene illustrates the suffering of those who have loved ones in uniform. It also presents another brief patch of sanity before the onslaught resumes.

Q Why do you think this chapter was included in the book?

Q Imagine a day in the life of the elderly woman and her family.

Chapter 11: 'Arras' (pp.165–85)

Summary: *The Canadian troops loot the deserted city of Arras; US troops arrive.*

This chapter is set in April 1918, the month of Germany's last major offensive, which brought the Allies into danger of defeat until the timely influx of fresh American troops and weapons helped to turn the tide. The Canadian troops are to be used as 'shock troops' to break the German offensive. By now, the soldiers have come to simply loathe the war – 'T'hell with the war', one curses (p.167). It is not hard to imagine mutiny occurring in the ranks, as happened in the French and Russian armies. Discussion follows about the monetary cost of the war and about war profiteers – of whom there are reckoned to be millions. 'There's two kinds of people in the world', remarks one man, 'those that like wars and those that fight 'em' (p.171). Between those two groups there is no common ground. Why is the war continuing, the men wonder, when no-one seems to want it to?

Key point

It is interesting to note that nowhere in this book is there any discussion of the politics of the war – these soldiers appear to have no quarrel with their German enemy.

The city of Arras, where the action of this chapter takes place, appears to be deserted. This makes it easy for the soldiers to move in and loot it. They take up residence in a deserted house and indulge themselves with good quality cigarettes, champagne and luxury foods. This is the incident that aroused so much anger from the many Canadian veterans who disputed its veracity.

Q Many Canadian veterans were offended by the suggestion that Canadian troops had looted Arras. How do you respond to the soldiers' behaviour? Can it be excused? What evidence of growing discontent among the troops is there in this chapter?

Q 'What the hell are we fightin' for, anyhow?' asks one soldier (p.182). To what extent is the lack of a sense of purpose at the heart of the soldiers' discontent?

Chapter 12: 'Vengeance' (pp.187–208)

Summary: *At the Battle of Amiens, hundreds of unarmed German soldiers are shot; Broadbent dies; the narrator is wounded in the foot and has to return home.*

Tactics have changed: there are to be no more human wave attacks, but short rushes instead. The narrator recalls a pep talk by a general who asks the men to avenge the German attack on the British ship, *Llandovery Castle*. One colonel implies that the men should take no prisoners, as 'we'll have to feed 'em out of our rations' (p.192). During the battle, hundreds of unarmed Germans approach, obviously trying to surrender, but they are killed in retaliation for the sinking of the ship – which, we soon learn, was carrying war materials.

Mercifully – that is how it feels – the narrator is wounded in exactly the right part of his body; he has finally achieved a 'Blighty' (a wound requiring repatriation). This is the greatest moment of relief in the entire book – he settles back in 'happy relief' (p.202) with a cigarette, knowing that his time in the war is over. However, this relief is mixed with a feeling of loss when the narrator witnesses the death of his comrade, Broadbent.

It is interesting to note a couple of vignettes in this chapter that stand apart from the rest of the narrative. One is the brief description of the battlefield before dawn: the only sounds are those of nature. Human beings seem to be the only blot on the landscape. The other is the moment when the wounded narrator watches the work of ants on their anthill. Even in this place of disorder, the processes of nature go on.

Q The narrator mentions the war poets and 'the poppies of which [they] are writing back home' (p.189). Study some of these poems. What does the poppy symbolise, even today?

Q 'An enemy like the Hun does not merit humane treatment' (p.191). Examine the role of propaganda in World War I.

CHARACTERS & RELATIONSHIPS

We need to recognise that the emphasis in this book is not so much on character development and the subtleties of relationships between characters as on the characters' all-encompassing struggle for survival. Growth and the development of the personality are usually impossible in circumstances of such disorder and strain. We see the characters in situations of extraordinary stress and distress, rather than in the wider range of situations we might encounter in a different work. The events of the war are so much more powerful than the personalities of the characters. Aspects of their personalities that would be on display in less traumatic circumstances are eclipsed.

Key point

To a large degree, these characters are representative types, rather than individuals in their own right. That is, many of the characters appear to have been created for the purpose of exemplifying a particular attitude to the war, a particular world view, or a particular quality or attribute.

The narrator is a possible exception to this. As he is at the centre of all events, relating them and commenting upon them, we are able to form a broader view of him than of any of the other characters. Nonetheless, he is in some ways typical of many soldiers in this war: perhaps his anonymity is intended to suggest this 'everyman' quality.

The narrator

The purpose of the anonymous narrator – we never learn his name – is to speak for the author, to put before us much of what the author wants to convey about the nature of the war. It is probably not too much to say that this character is based on Harrison himself and his personal war experiences. We can see, for example, that the narrator's experiences closely parallel Harrison's own, from the time of his enlistment in

Montreal to the time of his wounding at Amiens. The narrator puts before us an account of war that rings true because it comes from the author's firsthand experiences. We may indeed ask if it is possible for authors to write convincingly about war if they have not had direct experience of it. Most convincing narratives of war come from men who have had such experience: Stephen Crane's classic novel *The Red Badge of Courage* (1895) is a notable exception.

The narrator seems typical of many young men who fought in World War I. Like the youths of the Allied nations to whom Harrison dedicates his book, the narrator is 'bewildered' by the savagery of the war and is often overtaken by the events that confront him. He expresses a sense of incomprehension; he wants 'to catch hold of something … that will explain this mad fury, this maniacal congealed hatred that pours down on our heads' (p.27). Like all his comrades in arms, he feels terror and he often draws out of himself the courage to merely keep going from one minute to the next. There is something heroic about that.

The narrator gives us a very detailed picture of his physical suffering and that of his comrades: the crushing weight of exhaustion and of his boots and gear, the pain of physical ailments and wounds, the discomfort of filthy clothes and the intolerable irritation of lice. He resembles his comrades, too, in his longing for, and enjoyment of, simple pleasures such as a comfortable night's sleep and a cigarette to smoke in times of acute stress.

In these respects, we could describe the narrator as an ordinary soldier, if indeed there were 'ordinary' soldiers in this war, for merely to endure it to the end must have called upon extraordinary resources. Apart from his ability to endure, he has other admirable qualities. He has great courage, as his volunteering for the 'brigade raid' demonstrates, and he feels pride in having gone through that without cracking. Although he is capable of killing, he has a strong conscience that torments him when he looks back on the death of Karl. And he shows his conscience and his sense of compassion when he spares Karl's brother and treats him humanely. He recognises the basic humanity of his enemy. Furthermore, he clearly feels a sense of pity for the suffering civilians in the war zone, battered and bewildered as the fighting roars around them. He shares his precious tobacco with the elderly Frenchman who craves it. He is also kind to Renaud, the new recruit gripped by fear.

Another emotion that often seizes the narrator is a sense of anger at the mere fact of the war, and especially at the men who, from positions of safety, have sent him and so many others to risk their lives and their sanity. For him, it is these men who are the real enemy, not the Germans.

Brown

The lives of all the frontline soldiers in this book are miserable, but they are miserable in different ways. Brown's misery often stems from the fact that he is accident-prone, always snagging parts of his uniform on barbed wire, always in trouble with commanding officers such as Clark. He is a farmer's son, 'tall, awkward' (p.36) and not very bright. This makes him 'the butt for the ridicule of his mates and an object of hatred for [the malevolent] Clark' (p.36). His is a sad story: his experiences are particularly hard and then he is killed. He is so unfortunate that there is a kind of inevitability about his death, after which he becomes a symbol for the rest of the men. That is, he represents the fate that threatens them all. He is the only married member of the group and provides his mates with welcome stories of domestic pleasures. After his death, his wife, too, becomes a symbol – a symbol of the many women widowed by the war.

Broadbent

Brave, conscientious and aware of his position of responsibility (he is promoted to the rank of sergeant), Broadbent survives many trials until he is killed at the Battle of Amiens, at which the narrator is also wounded. He is a skilful soldier who maintains his composure and thinks quickly in circumstances that would paralyse many others. He fights aggressively and his aggression also surfaces in his feud over bread with Cleary (p.74). He tries to maintain order in the midst of the chaos that is always threatening: he tries to deflect mutinous talk (p.170); he tries to intervene in the dispute between Fry and Clark (p.154); and he is concerned about the consequences of the looting of Arras (p.178). He also displays the dry, black humour shared by many of the men, such as when he warns Anderson to stop praying aloud: 'don't tell God where you are or we'll all get killed' (p.150).

Fry

This man represents the soldier who reaches the end point of exhaustion and becomes both fatalistic and apparently indifferent to his fate: 'I'm going to get it this time ... And I don't care, either. I'm fed up' (p.142). The most significant act he commits is shooting his own captain, Clark, during an altercation (p.154). His initial defiance of Clark may have been prompted by feeling that he had nothing left to lose; shooting him may have arisen from the same feeling, or perhaps it was done simply out of self-defence, since Clark had already drawn his revolver. Like the other soldiers whose deaths are described in the book, he dies in a gruesome way.

Clark

This man is the type of officer few of the men would have been sorry to lose. Some of them seem to regard him as more of an enemy than the Germans themselves. What we are shown of the relationship between Clark and his men makes nonsense of the notion propagated by the newspapers at home that unity and high morale prevail among the men at the front. He is brutally unsympathetic to the suffering of his men, whether it takes the form of Fry's wounded arm, Brown's blundering or Renaud's fear. Contemptuously nicknamed 'White Breeches' by his men (p.36), he is the type of unpopular, tyrannical officer who can easily become a target of his men when tempers and discipline are frayed, so it is not altogether surprising that he meets his end in the way that he does. The fact that he is English also disadvantages him in the eyes of the men:

as Canadians, they feel that they are colonial cannon fodder for Britain. As one quips: 'Canada is under the lion's [England's] tail' (p.83).

Renaud

Renaud represents the soldier who loses his nerve under the stress of battle. Later, though, he seems to regain his composure and his face becomes 'red with excitement' (p.144). He is a sorrowful figure, 'an undersized French Canadian recruit' (p.139) who is demonstrably unfit. The narrator is at a loss to know 'how he ever passed the doctor' (p.139). Probably by this stage of the war the demand for men was so acute that many such men were passed as fit for service. He suffers greatly both from physical pain and from terror, which threaten to overwhelm him at a critical moment. He meets a horrible death in battle.

Anderson

We hear quite a lot from Anderson in the course of the narrative and what he says is almost always to do with the subject of God and the need to invoke his protective powers. He is to a large extent a caricature, as he believes in the kind of God who will protect the men if only they pray hard enough. His belief that the war will end on 1 August 1917, a belief that he derives from the Bible (p.83), is both eccentric and absurd, the kind of belief that might be held by a member of a marginal religious sect.

The author uses Anderson to discredit the view – often held by religious fundamentalists – that morality is essentially to do with matters such as sexual behaviour and refraining from swearing. Clearly, those who hold such beliefs have little grasp of what might define a truly moral life. It is hard to deny, for example, that war itself is a far greater evil than swearing or any form of consensual sexual behaviour could ever be.

The Anglican curate

World War I was the last major war during which mainstream Christian clergy widely sought to invoke God's blessing. This war, of course, became so horrible that relatively few clergy since have tried to enlist God in war. It is clear that Harrison has written the character of the clergyman into his book in order to condemn the role of those clergy who, like this character, sought to depict the war as a holy struggle that deserved the blessing of God. Such men appeared conveniently to have forgotten the teachings of Jesus that we should love our enemies, and that the peacemakers are blessed. Harrison's clergyman is a 'fighting parson' (p.133), but he will never have to get any blood on his hands. His view that the war has 'brought out the most heroic qualities of the common people' (p.134) is also discredited.

It is interesting to compare Harrison's views of Christian clergy during the war with those found in other works of protest by veterans, such as the poetry of Wilfred Owen and Siegfried Sassoon. Both these men made Christian clergy the object of bitter derision. The accuracy of Harrison's portrait of the Anglican curate can be attested through accounts such as this one:

> On Easter Sunday, 4th April 1915, Dean Inge preached at St Paul's Cathedral. After a man who vociferously protested against the war had been bundled out of the congregation, the Dean read [Rupert] Brooke's sonnet *'If I should die, think only this of me'*, and ventured to suggest that this young soldier should take rank with 'our greatest poets.'[17]

The civilians in Montreal and London

The narrator shows us two main groups of civilians living in countries outside the war zone. In each case, we are shown these people's

[17] Robert Giddings, *The War Poets*, Bloomsbury, London, 1990, p.37.

ignorance about the true nature of the war. Although none of these characters are presented in any depth, their inclusion in the narrative is vital in revealing the narrator's attitudes. The first group comprise the women of Montreal who are 'hysterical' with excitement as they farewell the troops (p.16). As the men depart, the women are 'singing and cheering' (p.17). This incongruous behaviour is consistent with many other accounts of the civilian response to the departure of troops, especially in the early years of the war, when the soldiers were often farewelled to the accompaniment of brass bands and songs. It is as if the troops are going off to take part in a sporting contest, rather than to a slaughterhouse.

The second group are the civilians in London, whom the narrator observes while he is on leave in that city. His contempt for these people runs too deep for words: 'I cannot formulate my hatred of these people' (p.126). The contrast between the men at the front and the people safe back home could not be starker. It is as if they are living in a different world (or even on a different planet). The brief description of the 'jolly-faced rotund civilian' at the theatre who glibly whispers the word 'shell-shocked' (p.126) to his female companion to explain the narrator's response to his question is a sharply observed and telling moment.

Gladys

This woman – 'that delightful combination of wife, mother, and courtesan' (p.130) – is the only civilian in London who is presented in a favourable light. She is the embodiment of qualities that any soldier on leave would wish to find: softness, warmth and nurturance. The type of relationship that Gladys and the narrator share would have been common in wartime, when many soldiers would have been seeking a short-term relationship with a woman with no strings attached. In the circumstances under which such men were living, they would have had to take love and affection wherever they could find them.

Gladys is obviously a sympathetic and kind woman (even her name sounds maternal) and she gives the narrator the sort of company that helps him to forget the war, which she thoughtfully does not mention. (Other civilians, by contrast, ply the narrator with questions about it.) Gladys is experienced in her role of offering love and comfort to soldiers. Interestingly, she never addresses the narrator by name, but calls him 'boy' instead, indicating both her awareness of his tenderness of years and her reluctance to become too emotionally involved with him.

The civilians in the war zone

Many of the French civilians are shadowy figures, drawn by the author with quick, sharp brushstrokes. The dominant impression he creates is of their suffering: the degree to which they have been beaten down by circumstances and rendered hapless victims of the war that rages around them. The people in the town of Béthune, for example, are said to have the 'peculiar stunted walk of human moles' (p.108). Because they have suffered, they are often compassionate towards the soldiers. The narrator offers a couple of vignettes showing this, such as the one that introduces the old woman who tenderly bathes his foot, while consoling him with the words, 'my poor one' ('*mon pauvre*' in French, p.160).

THEMES & ISSUES

The impact of war on humans

This matter is obviously central to the book; at every stage the author seeks to reveal the ways in which the combatants in the war are damaged by it. The book is filled with images of the terrors of war, many of them gruesome. In particular, Harrison shows us that a soldier's senses are placed under constant siege. Apart from the horrific sights, there is the constant, overwhelming noise of battle, the smells of the trenches, the itchy irritation caused by lice, and the pain of wounds. It is little wonder that there were many psychiatric casualties as a result of this war from which many men never recovered. Their distress was glibly categorised by the blanket term 'shell shock', whereas the nature of that distress could well have been as individual and as varied as the men themselves. Pat Barker's *Regeneration Trilogy* demonstrates this complexity.

Under these conditions, life is lived from moment to moment, with no assurance of any long-term future. The struggle merely to survive overwhelms all else; such as when the narrator tells of the way men fight each other over a piece of bread. Cleary and Broadbent attack each other 'like hungry, snarling animals' (p.74). In a similar image of savagery, the narrator later describes how he and his men regress to the level of 'snarling, savage beasts' (p.148) in their fight to the death with the enemy.

Courage and the resilience of the human spirit

Key quote

> 'I am proud of myself. I have been tested and found not wanting.' (p.98)

The narrator makes this statement after the 'brigade raid' for which he volunteers. While it is easy to demonstrate the depths to which men can sink during war, it is hard not to admire their endurance under intolerable circumstances, as well as their other positive qualities such as courage in the face of overwhelming terror. There can be little doubt that the politicians and generals running the war took advantage of that courage to no good end. Yet that courage was truly heroic – whether it was manifested through enormously brave deeds, or simply in the capacity to laugh and to appreciate humour. It is remarkable that often the human spirit cannot be extinguished, even in the slaughterhouse of war.

Key point

An interesting aspect of the book is the way the narrator, in spite of everything, is still able to appreciate the everyday beauties and rhythms of nature, whether these are found in the fresh taste and smell of a piece of mud, in the beauty of the stars overhead or in the work of ants going about their daily business.

Differing attitudes to war

Key quote

'There's two kinds of people in this world – there's those that like wars and those that fight 'em, pal.' (p.171)

The above comment from an anonymous 'mutinous grumbler' (p.170) tersely expresses the attitude of many soldiers, including the narrator. If these soldiers ever entertained any hope of experiencing glory in war, it is quickly shot down on the battlefield. The dominant aim of most of the combatants is merely to survive and to resume their lives at home. It is interesting to note that there is almost no talk of a motive for fighting or of the politics of the war. There is no real sense that the sacrifice is in the service of any worthy goal. The soldiers appear to be victims at the mercy of events quite beyond their control, concerned only with their own survival. Nor is there any real hostility towards the German enemy. The soldiers 'never refer to the Germans as [their] enemy' (p.39), and when the narrator kills Karl, for example, he feels nothing so much as a sense of sorrow at the death of another human being.

Indeed, the book asks the question: who really *is* the enemy? If it is not the Germans, then most likely it is the politicians who have sent the men to the war in the first place and the war profiteers who are happy to see it continue. Or it could be incompetent officers: those who were led by such men were widely described at the time as 'lions led by donkeys'. The enemy also consists of those English civilians who are living in comfortable ignorance of what is really happening across the Channel, such as the man at the theatre, with his facile dismissal of the narrator's blank stare as 'shell shock' (p.126).

The home front

Key quote

'I cannot formulate my hatred of these people.' (p.126)

The narrator's emphasis on the incomprehension of English civilians raises an interesting issue. How accurate is his portrayal of civilian attitudes to the war? How much did civilians really know about what was happening at the front? Were they in denial of a reality of which they were aware, or were they simply uninformed? Or did the propaganda offensive which demonised Germany as a mortal enemy – 'The only good German is a dead German' ran one slogan – succeed in its aims? Certainly, a war fever was whipped up in England – and presumably in Germany, too – and the patriotic mood of the time was fully exploited. Men were encouraged to enlist through the playing of jingoistic popular songs such as 'We don't want to lose you, but we think you ought to go/For your King and Country both need you so'. In one of his letters, the writer DH Lawrence lamented that 'it seems as if we were all going to be dragged into the *danse macabre*' (dance of death), concluding that 'my dear nation is bitten by the tarantula, and the venom has gone home at last'.[18]

We are familiar these days with the word 'spin' – the presentation of information with a slant designed to obscure the truth. No doubt an earlier form of 'spin' was created by the propagandists of wartime. *Generals Die in Bed* strongly suggests that there was an enormous gap between the views about the war of the soldiers actually fighting the war

---

[18] DH Lawrence, *Selected Letters*, Penguin, Harmondsworth, 1950, p.102.

and those of the civilians in England. The turning of the war into a subject for theatrical farce, for example, appears quite obscene.

Reading *Generals Die in Bed*, as well as other works about the war, I often found myself wondering how such massive slaughter was allowed to continue with little or no protest at home. Would patriotism alone have been sufficient to allow civilians to tolerate news of a death toll that eventually touched almost every family? Or did officialdom wilfully keep people in ignorance? We know, for example, that:

> Up until the end of the Somme battle in 1916, the *Daily Telegraph* and *Morning Post* printed the names of all casualties but after the Somme (during which casualties varied between 1000 and 5000 a day), only the officers' casualty lists were published. Understandably, attitudes at home changed as weeks turned into months, 1914 merged into 1915, and years went by. People grew to be more matter-of-fact about receiving news of death, as it became more and more of a seeming inevitability.
>
> The cinema was an important means of conveying to those at home some idea of active service abroad. In the early years of the war, newsreels showed high jinks at camp, jolly singsongs, and men playing football. It was not until after the Somme that the public saw actual footage of men going over the top and getting shot or wounded (although there is some controversy about the authenticity of this footage).[19]

Whatever the media coverage of the war, we can be quite sure that such coverage was far more limited than is the media coverage of wars today, when footage from war zones is flashed around the world as it happens and turned into instant history. We know that media coverage of the Vietnam War, for example, played a major role in galvanising opposition to that war, and we may speculate that, had television been available

---

[19] Robert Giddings, *The War Poets*, p.21.

during World War I, such coverage would have had a similar effect on the civilian public then. (Television became widespread after the end of the 1940s.)

The sacrifice of the young by the old

Key quote

'Old soldiers never die – young ones do.' (American protest poster)

This variation upon the adage made famous by General Douglas MacArthur, 'Old soldiers never die, they just fade away', trenchantly speaks of the sad reality of all wars. That is, it is the young who are sacrificed by the old in wars. There is always an especially acute poignancy in the loss of so many young men – often no more than boys – cut off before they have had a chance to live their lives.

The scene in Chapter 5 in which the soldiers on rest from the war bathe in a nearby stream highlights the contrast between the youthfulness of their bodies – 'slim, hard, graceful' (p.68) – and the 'weather-beaten and ... aged look' (p.69) that long months in the trenches have stamped on their faces. The scene in which these soldiers splash boyishly in the water is also poignant because we are reminded of the vulnerability of those bodies, which are being 'fattened up' for the slaughter to come.

The emphasis on the blighting of youth is a leitmotif (recurring theme) in the text. The narrator maintains a steady focus on the effects of war upon youth. The 'lads' from the French village where the soldiers bathe 'have the faces of little old men' (p.69). The two Germans whom the narrator takes prisoner during the brigade raid are boys of about seventeen, their extreme youth grotesquely highlighted by their ill-fitting uniforms (p.92).

Key point

We may speculate about the lasting effects of the war, not just on the bodies of these youths, but on their minds. After all, they are being subjected constantly to stresses great enough to cripple men of far greater age and experience. For many of these young men, soldiering would have been their first real job and, like the young soldiers of all wars, they may well have come to feel distress that this job required them to be hired killers.

Alongside these images of the young, Harrison places images of older men, who live protected from the onslaught. The narrator depicts unforgivingly these generals who 'die in bed'. The first one we meet is 'A little grey-haired man' (p.111) who is greeted with a pomp and ceremony far removed from the lives of most men serving below him. The second makes a bombastic speech in which he dehumanises the Germans and urges revenge to be taken against them. And then we are also aware of other older men at home whose actions are prolonging the war – the war profiteers and the politicians. We are told little of the activities of the politicians and the generals, but it is not hard to conclude that their conduct of the war is disastrous. No doubt Harrison would have kept in his mind the well-known comment that the British soldiers were 'lions led by donkeys', and examples of those 'donkeys' spring readily to mind. The generals of World War I were recklessly wasteful of their soldiers' lives; during the tenure of the egregious French general Nivelle, for example, mass mutinies occurred in the ranks of the French army. In *Generals Die in Bed*, we are made aware of the stirrings of such discontent among the frontline soldiers.

The persistence of war in human life

Every work of anti-war protest at least implicitly asks us to consider the question: why has war persisted in human affairs from the beginning of recorded history? What is there in our make-up that leads us to resort to the Stone Age barbarism detailed in Harrison's work? The narrator wishes to tell his German prisoner that 'something took us both … and dumped us into a lonely, shrieking hole at night' (p.95). What exactly is that something, and from where does it come? In another scene, the narrator feels that the shock of battle produces a sense of cosmic disorder, as if '[a]n insane god is pounding [the trench] with Cyclopean fists, madly, incessantly' (p.77). And yet this madness surely comes from within human beings themselves, doesn't it? The novel ultimately reminds us that, as Frederic Manning observed in his author's note to his novel *Her*

Privates We, 'War is waged by men; not by beasts, or by gods. It is a peculiarly human activity'.[20]

The role of the anti-war writer

Key quote

'They have no business to forget. They should be made to remember.' (p.125)

It is difficult to imagine anything of much value arising from the vast waste and destruction of a war such as the one of which Harrison writes. And yet, we can argue that veterans of that war who became writers aimed to salvage something of value from that dark experience by registering their own anger and revulsion. By doing so, such writers are seeking to help prevent the recurrence of war. When the narrator tells Gladys that the English civilians 'have no right to forget' about the war, but instead 'They should be made to remember' (p.125), he is implicitly endorsing the saying by the philosopher George Santayana: 'those who cannot remember the past are condemned to repeat it'.[21] The writings of anti-war soldiers such as Owen and Sassoon were, of course, not sufficient to prevent World War II or the wars that have followed it, but they certainly shocked with their uncompromising descriptions of what they had witnessed. There can be little doubt that such writers strongly contributed to the widespread reluctance to take up arms again in 1939, and to the much greater care that British commanders showed towards the lives of their soldiers in the war that began in that year.

---

[20] Cited in Robin Gerster, *Big-Noting: the heroic theme in Australian war writing*, Melbourne University Press, Carlton, 1992, p.245.

[21] *Bloomsbury Thematic Dictionary of Quotations*, p.176.

The struggle to maintain basic humanity

Key quote

'Who can describe the few moments of peace and sunshine in a soldier's life? The animal pleasure in feeling the sun on a naked body. The cool, caressing, lapping water. The feeling of security, of deep inward happiness ...' (p.69)

What positive values does the narrator affirm in the midst of a war in which the combatants are often reduced to the level of feral animals or prehistoric men? It would be easy to describe the view of life that Harrison presents as unrelievedly negative, yet we can discern a few glimpses of something more positive.

Key point

While the essential struggle of the men is simply to stay alive, we are also shown that there might be things worth staying alive for.

I am thinking of those simple pleasures that can bring comfort in times of great stress, such as the cigarettes, wine, good food and comfortable beds that the soldiers enjoy in their times of respite. These ordinary pleasures are enhanced in the midst of great stress.

Of even more importance is the maintenance of the basic humanity that the narrator demonstrates when he spares his German prisoners, weeps over the death of Karl, tries to help Renaud in his time of great fear, and shares his precious tobacco with the elderly Frenchman. And then there is the goodness and generosity of the French civilians who offer comfort and care to the soldiers.

QUESTIONS & ANSWERS

The essay topics below show a range of possible styles and formats, and are suitable for senior English assessment tasks and examinations.

Essay topics

1 'It is the way in which Harrison creates a sense of the mood and atmosphere of life in the war zone that holds our attention most strongly.'
To what extent do you agree?

2 How do conditions in the trenches make life a living hell for the characters?
Refer to two or three characters in your answer.

3 'The narrator's unrelenting description of the horrors of war shows only the dark side of human nature.'
Discuss.

4 Why are the civilians in *Generals Die in Bed* unable to understand the sufferings of the soldiers at the front?

5 'Harrison's distinctive style of writing helps to illustrate the reality of life in the trenches.'
Discuss.

6 'Harrison's chief purpose in writing *Generals Die in Bed* was clearly to create a strongly anti-war work.'
Discuss.

7 '*Generals Die in Bed* shows that heroism and glory are never possible in war.'
Discuss.

8 '*Generals Die in Bed* warns of the drastic consequences of resorting to violence as a means of settling disputes.'
Discuss.

9 '*Generals Die in Bed* demonstrates that some stresses are too terrible for humans to tolerate.'
Discuss.

10 '*Generals Die in Bed* suggests that those in positions of power have little concern for those over whom they exercise that power.'
Discuss.

11 '*Generals Die in Bed* shows that humans are totally dehumanised by war.'
Discuss.

12 '*Generals Die in Bed* demonstrates that it is those who make wars, not those who fight them, who deserve our condemnation.'
Discuss.

Analysing a sample topic

'*Generals Die in Bed* shows the reader that heroism and glory are never possible in war.' Discuss.

You can argue this topic in different ways while following the same basic pattern. There is no doubt that your work will benefit if you set yourself up with a well-structured and reasonably detailed plan. Such a plan will save you time in writing up your essay and give you the confidence that comes from having a clear sense of direction.

- Begin by identifying the key words and phrases from the prompt. In your opening paragraph, define those key words, 'heroism' and 'glory'. Don't do this by reaching into your dictionary and writing something like 'the Macquarie Dictionary defines heroism as the doing of brave and outstanding deeds'. Instead, contextualise your definition by writing something like: 'Merely to endure day-to-day life in the trenches of France demanded remarkable courage and bravery, or heroism, from the soldiers'. By doing this, we have begun to define the key word while at the same time setting up the beginnings of an argument.
- Gather together in note form all the material from the text that is relevant to the question, then compartmentalise that material –

divide it into sections that will then become your paragraphs. At the planning stages, it's important to build structure into your material.

- Remember that you are not required simply to agree with the prompt. Argue with it, reframe it as you see fit. You might, for example, argue that while heroism was possible, glory was not.
- Avoid beginning with formulations such as, 'I totally agree with this statement'. This is mere assertion; instead, every sentence you write should be part of a developing argument.
- If you get stuck, bring your mind back to the characters; this will bring to your mind relevant material that will help you deal with the question.

How to structure your essay

- Aim to develop a consistent argument about the statement.
- Begin with a strong opening paragraph that telescopes down the main ideas you will develop later.
- The first paragraph should be fairly general, signposting the direction in which your argument will go. Make sure, however, that you address all the key terms of the topic here. Focus on the text itself from the outset.
- In your subsequent paragraphs, work from the general to the specific. Work in plenty of illustrative detail from the text. Quotations can help, but keep them short and integrate them with your own words as much as possible.
- Establish strong links between all the paragraphs of your essay. Use linking words and phrases; use a key word from the last sentence of one paragraph in the first sentence of the next. Do everything you can to build continuity.
- Good topic sentences throughout will help you stay on track. It is also a good idea to have one sentence in each paragraph that relates directly to the question.
- In your final paragraph, you need a strong reiteration of your main argument, but without simply repeating yourself. Aim for a decisive, conclusive statement.

SAMPLE ANSWER

"In this flickering light this German and I enact our tragedy."

How does *Generals Die in Bed* win our support equally for both Germans and the Allied soldiers?

Charles Yale Harrison depicts both German and Allied infantrymen as dispensable, minor players in the gruesome theatre of the Great War. In the quotation above, Harrison uses the words of drama to describe the horrific situation of the two soldiers; they 'enact' a 'tragedy' that is directed by unseen and, as Harrison would have it, brutal forces. Harrison does indeed win our support for the equally hapless German and Allied soldiers but he is scathing in his treatment of the commanders who dehumanise these men and send them to their deaths as casually as if they were actors in a play. It is the authenticity of the first-person narrative which is most effective in gaining the reader's sympathy for the infantrymen on both sides of the war, but we are also persuaded of the unrelenting horror of their situation by the spare nature of the writing, its cool and, at times, sardonic tone and the focus on the ruined landscape and the soldiers' broken physical condition.

Harrison employs the first-person narrative to gain immediacy in his account of World War I. The protagonist is not a thinker, he does not enlist for any clear reason and neither he nor his comrades explore what the war might be about. In the same way that the protagonist shows no real understanding of why he is going to war, once in the trenches he expresses no real animosity towards the Germans; like the Allied soldiers, they are the 'hundreds of men ... standing a mile or two from me pulling gun lanyards, blowing us to smithereens. I know that and nothing else'. This first-person account of the experience of war is highly personal, full of feeling but not all-knowing; in fact, Harrison is contemptuous of third-person accounts of the war provided by journalists and newspapers which purport to tell the truth about the war. His experiences in London where the war is either made comedic in a musical or used as the subject of a pious homily by a priest cause him to feel disgusted. The truth of the war for the protagonist is that the 'infantrymen on both sides suffer, are killed, wounded'. Unlike the generals' speeches and the propaganda produced by the newspapers, Harrison knows it is not the Germans who are his foes: 'We have learned who our enemies are – the lice, some of the officers, and Death'.

Complementing this refusal to accept the sophistry of the talk about the reasons for war is a strong physicality to Harrison's writing; it is the everyday experience of the trenches that provides the truth in this text. Harrison conveys the claustrophobia of the trenches and the profound and shattering insistence of bombardments: '[t]he air is thick with the pale yellow smoke of high explosives – the colour of boarding house tea. I feel a warm trickle on the sides of my neck. My ears are bleeding from the force and fury of the detonation'. The reader, like the soldier, is not made conscious of the reasons for the war, but Harrison ensures that we feel and see its vicious effects, and experience through his writing the unrelenting noise and horror in which both sides are captured.

Perhaps the most disturbing incident in the text is the moment when the protagonist kills a German with his bayonet and they enact their tragedy, because at this moment Harrison faces a real person and one whom he does not see as his true enemy but a fellow victim. The image of the German's boyish face and downy cheeks brings into close focus the enormity of the murder he commits and reveals the lie that it is this man who is his enemy.

The final words of this episode are spoken by a German who points to the battlefield – 'his trenches and ours, the thundering artillery, the funkhole' – and says, '*es ist schrecklich – schrecklich* [awful]'. Harrison thus emphasises the shared tragedy of German and Allied infantrymen alike.

REFERENCES & READING

The text

Harrison, Charles Yale, *Generals Die in Bed*, Penguin, Camberwell, Victoria, 2003. First published in 1930.

Books and articles

Barker, Pat, *The Regeneration Trilogy: Regeneration, The Eye in the Door, The Ghost Road*, Penguin, London, 1991, 1993 and 1995 respectively.

Bloomsbury Thematic Dictionary of Quotations, 1997.

Carruth, Hayden, ed., *The Voice that is Great Within Us – American poetry of the twentieth century*, Bantam Books, New York, 1970.

Crane, Stephen, *The Red Badge of Courage* D. Appleton & Co., New York, 1895.

Edelman, Bernard, ed., *Dear America – letters home from Vietnam*, Norton, London, 2002 First published 1985.

Fussell, Paul, *The Great War and Modern Memory*, Oxford University Press, New York and London, 1977. First published in 1975.

Gerster, Robin, *Big-Noting: the heroic theme in Australian war writing*, Melbourne University Press, Carlton, Vic., 1992.

Giddings, Robert, *The War Poets*, Bloomsbury, London, 1990.

Graves, Robert, *Goodbye to All That*, Penguin, Ringwood, 1969. First published in 1929.

Hemingway, Ernest, *A Farewell to Arms*, Charles Scribner's Sons, New York, 1929.

Hollis, Matthew & Paul Keegan, eds, *101 Poems Against War*, Faber and Faber, London, 2003.

James, Leonard F, *Western Man and the Modern World: Book 3: Industrialism, Imperialism, and War*, Pergamon Press, Sydney, 1973.

Jones, Barry, *Decades of Decision, 1860–: a compendium of modern history*, Horwitz Publications, Sydney, 1965.

Lawrence, DH, *Selected Letters*, Penguin, Harmondsworth, 1950.

Manning, Frederic, *Her Privates We,* Serpent's Tail, London 1999. First published in 1929.

O'Brien, Tim, *The Things They Carried*, Collins, London, 1990.

Owen, Wilfred, *The Collected Poems of Wilfred Owen*, Day Lewis, C, ed., Chatto and Windus, London, 1977. First published in 1963.

Parsons, IM, ed., *Men Who March Away: poems of the First World War*, The Hogarth Press, London, 1987.

Prior, Robin & Wilson, Trevor, *The First World War*, Cassell, London, 2001. First published in 1999.

Remarque, Erich Maria, *All Quiet on the Western Front*, Pan Books, London, 1987. First published in 1929.

Sassoon, Siegfried, *The Old Huntsman and Other Poems*, William Heinemann, London, 1917.

——*Memoirs of a Fox-hunting Man*, Faber and Faber, London, 1960. First published in 1928.

——*Memoirs of an Infantry Officer*, Faber and Faber, London, 1989. First published in 1930.

Stallworthy, Jon, ed., *The Oxford Book of War Poetry*, Oxford University Press, Oxford and New York, 1984. Reprinted in 1990.

Taylor, AJP, *The First World War*, Penguin, London, 1966.

——*From Sarejevo to Potsdam*, Thames and Hudson, London, 1966.

Thich Nhat Hanh, *Call Me By My True Names*, Parallax Press, Albany, California, 1999.

Tuchman, Barbara, *The Guns of August*, Ballantine Books, New York, 1994. First published in 1962.

Vance, J, *The Formation of Historical Consciousness: a case study in literature*, University of British Columbia, 2001.